GUS

BY G. S. WILLIS

"Based on True Events"

From

The Book of Willis

Credits

Cover art by: Kristina Wheeat
Cover Designs by: Hayley Faye of fayefayedesigns
Cover Designs by: design_desk
Book Interior Design and Layout by:

raselkhondokar

Paperback ISBN: 978-1-7339133-0-0
eBook ISBN: 978-1-7339133-1-7

Printed in USA by 48HrBooks
www.48HrBooks.com

Acknowledgements

Thanks to my family, and to my Brothers and Sisters who were always supportive. To my Mom who nurtured me and pushed me to achieve. To my Dad for always being there, especially during those times that I didn't realize he was watching over me.

Thanks to my friends, various readers, beta readers and editors who encouraged and motivated me with their interest and feedback to share this story.

To Alan my friend, who was my writing and southern dialogue consultant for his contributions. And for pushing me past my perfectionisms to get the story published.

To Mr. Hotchkiss my eighth grade English teacher at West Jr. High School. Who in making his annual class predictions of his student's prospective futures, planted the thought in my head that I would become a writer. Though I filed it away at the time, it would resurface time and again. Seemingly to almost follow me on my path. Hopefully this is the beginning of the journey Mr. Hotchkiss envisioned.

Table of Contents

INTRODUCTION

Being born in 1920's Depression-era Mississippi is a hard life. It was even harder if you were Black. Gus was a child born of two worlds. With a black mother and a white father, the law of the times dictated access to one and not the other.

Though he has a loving family, ongoing tensions between him and his mother push Gus to make a critical decision. At twelve years old unbeknownst to his family, Gus leaves home early one morning, long before the rooster crows. But he is not prepared for the dangers and life-threatening encounters that unfold. Being alone and Black in 1930's Jim Crow Mississippi could often feel like being the hunted. Gus's struggle to survive spark an awakening of his latent extrasensory gifts. Sleeping abilities that help to guide him; but all life lessons come at a cost. Will the lessons learned be enough to save him?

PROLOGUE

What do we keep... what do we forget?

I think I really began to understand my dad... the day we had an argument. Harsh words were exchanged, and I left in a huff for undergraduate school at Western Michigan University. My younger brother looked on hush mouthed as our disagreement became heated. I barked back at my dad in response. It was a first for me. I was leaving for college, looking for my independence, and taking all my stuff with me. I hurriedly finished the rest of my packing in silence. At eighteen or nineteen looking forward, life looks different than it does when looking back. Who among us doesn't feel empowered at that age, thinking we know the world and what is best as far as we are concerned.

Especially where parents are involved. I must confess that I did.

I left immediately after our spat, angry and unyielding, a sense of finality to my departure. Thus, I walked out that day with angry last words between us.

Hours later, after I arrived at school some three hours or so afterwards, I unpacked.

Ring, Ring!

The telephone chimed. It was my beloved, favorite sister calling me, "What did you say to Daddy? He was in tears!" she asked waiting for my response.

Speechless, I offered up nothing in response, shrugging my shoulders like a kid on the other end of the phone.

I was taken aback. This man of few words who always seemed so strong was crying because of me. I couldn't believe it, and even more, I couldn't bear that I might be responsible for it.

A short time after that, my mom called me, wanting to get to the bottom of things.

I'm quite sure my mom and sister, both tag-teamed me that day to find out what they could. But like most of the men in my family, I was not really sharing.

After a moment of silence, her voice softened. "Son," she said, "listen." And then she began to share with me a story of the early days of my dad's life. A story that put me on a path to enlightenment and understanding of the man that was my father.

* * *

So, it was that he was born into this life, unwelcome. Though the prevailing belief of the time was that children are resilient and they will recover from such things. Are our truly most damaging moments merely edited out, a trauma-blocking mind trick sheltering us from our most offending memories? One has to wonder the impact a negative birthing event has on a child and what that child may keep. Coming into this world feeling, intense anger, and hostility. Extreme negative emotions focused clearly on you. Will such fractured-memories and feelings, imprint on a child in ways unforeseen? Even more, will that child pass on his birth demons to others or even to his or her own children. If it is true that we are connected, then does such a connection hold fast even in our genetic memories, deep down to our very core?

This was my Dad's introduction into this life.

The following is my retelling of his story as was told to me by my mother and to the best of my ability, to remain true to the substance of it.

GENESIS

And so, his story began. On a stormy night in a small town in Mississippi, that August Willis, or Gus as he would come to be known, was born to a Black mother Addie Mae, and a White father. Such things were taboo, back then. Especially in the south, in the heart of a racist Mississippi culture that routinely hung young black men. Often for no reason other than a whim. To Addie, their union was never consensual. Yet, she kept it from her own father.

Upon seeing what appeared to him to be a white child, Addie's dad was so shocked, angry and hurt that he immediately grabbed the baby Gus and raced outside with child in hand. Amidst the rain, lightning and booming thunder that shook the skies that night, he raised his baby grandson over his head, to throw him down into the well below.

He stood over the well, the baby over his head.

"Please don't do this!" Addie clutched at his clothing, begging her father not to take the baby's life.

"Please." She murmured, her tears mixing in with the rain as she tugged at his blue jean overalls.

At long last hearing her words, he looked at his daughter, and then at the baby. He shook his head and stepped away from the well. His shoulders slumped, and he handed the child to his daughter. Then, without another word, he walked away, head down.

Whimpering, "Thank you," as he walked away, a sobbing Addie held the baby close, wrapping him up.

He would later confess to being thankful that he was prevented from doing such a foolish and cruel thing. It was an act that could not have been taken back. The blood of an innocent child on his hands would have haunted him. I do not claim to have known my great grandfather but I'm fairly certain, it was not something he could have lived with.

Both Addie and Gus sat crying after returning to the safety of the house.

* * *

Years passed, and Addie Mae, known to all as Addie, had other children. The youngest was born when Gus was eight. Gus was unique among his siblings–the only one born of a white father.

The kids fought often, as brothers and sisters do, but at the end of the day, they were family.

Life was hard on the farm, but they pulled together to make it work. During those depression era times, it was tough for many trying to make ends meet. There on the farm and for much of the country.

But all families have their problems. Whether Addie was aware of it or not Gus felt the anger and hidden resentment toward him. Things unsaid and disapproving looks, that crept out from her actions, at times left him feeling uncertain and insecure. As if he had at once been hit by an icy chill breeze. The resulting shudder gave him reason to pause, wondering what he could have done.

Looking at him Addie saw the face of his father and old feelings more times than not, resurfaced. She was sixteen, several months shy of seventeen when he was born. Unmarried and practically a child herself she had to suffer through her own indignities.

"What you doing with that White baby, girl?" White passers-by, demanded of her and her sister Lily as she stood at their roadside mailbox with Gus on her hip. She got mixed reactions from the men upon finding out the baby was hers but the women could be hateful.

"Hmph, some coon lover having some fun Ah guess," one lady who saw them together said cruelly. Her words and icy stare frightened Addie and made her feel unnerved. It prompted her to hold her baby close. The lady's' two-faced smile told Addie that she and Gus might not be safe around this woman. After that Gus stayed on the porch, where he was not visible from the road. When the mail needed checking, Addie or Lily would take turns going to the mailbox while the other stayed with the baby.

As Gus grew, being the oldest, he had a responsibility to look after his younger siblings and his mother. It was the way of things then.

But it was at the age of twelve some months after the death of his stepfather, his mom's misplaced anger and resentment pushed him to a crossroads. To the point of leaving home.

"Ah can't take this no more, Mama," Gus declared, confronting her. "What have Ah done to you?"

Addie, all five-feet-two-inches of her, stood as straight and still as an unmoving statue. Her quiet scrunched up expression was unrelenting.

"Do you want me to go, Mama?" Soft eyes peered up looking for any glimmer of hope. "You don't want me?"

"If you wanna leave, ain't nobody stopping' ya!" she replied curtly, her eyes tightening, as she crossed her arms.

Inside him, the weight of that biting reply sent a shudder and a loud, erratic thump through his body. It broke his heart. "Okay, mama, if you don't want me aroun' no more," he said slowly lowering his head, trying to hide his unsteady legs. Fragments of feelings, of images past, colors and sounds he did not recognize swelled up inside him, as if trying to surface and make themselves whole. Their presence only deepened his insecurities, as he struggled to get the next words out. "Ah'll be leavin' then," he said. Speaking the words so softly they seemed to run together.

Both walked away hurt and angry that day. For Gus however, the weight of it all was too much. Emotions overtook him and amidst them an intense feeling of being unwanted he could not shake.

He stepped outside, walking down the unpainted worn wooden steps and off the porch into the yard. Murmuring words that only he could hear. "Ain't changing. Ain't changing none at all." He kicked at a nearby bush as he crossed the yard. The frenzied cackles of a yard bird resting under the bush caught him by surprise as it scurried away flapping its wings. He recognized her, it was one of their best egg-laying hens. Gus did an about-face toward the house but seeing no one, abruptly turned back, to resume his original course. His heated breaths were fast and shallow as he trudged off toward the soft earth of the cornfields.

Should Ah go? He thought. "Just as well," and answered himself. "Just go on. Find me...

someplace else." *She don't want me aroun', ah don't wanna be here,* his thoughts told him.

In his heart, he knew it would not be that simple. Instead, he made his way from one side of the two-acre cornfield to the other and back, fighting with himself all the way as he tried to sort things out. Gradually his breathing slowed but the anger and hurt inside would not go away. At days end after quietly finishing his work, he was back home and asleep in his bed.

As he awoke that evening hearing the stirring of his brothers, he knew there was no going back but held onto a small hope. Alone in a darkened corner of the room, he shared with them, resolutely he made his plans that night.

Gus and Addie were both sorry later for what was said but as often is the case with harsh words and actions, the invisible wounds take time to heal. His temperament didn't help either. After years of deflecting his mom's anger, he had become a little sensitive to her criticisms.

Late that night, he moved secretly about and packed his knapsack. It was an old civil war soldier's haversack he had found and held on to. The haversack had been designed for soldiers to pack and carry their gear as they traveled. Gus never anticipated having to use it for this purpose.

Later as he sat quietly, alone on the porch, Will, alerted by Gus's silent movements, approached.

All who knew him, claimed Will to be an old soul. Being the second eldest, he and Gus had grown up closely. Will stood just shy of where Gus quietly sat, looking down at him. His piercing, seemingly ever-present gaze once locked in, beamed into your soul, often seeing more than he chose to reveal.

"Uh, ... been sort of a tough day," Will said softly... uncomfortably. His next words seemed to cause him pain. "Been feelin' kinda funny today Gus. Scared even. But don't know why." He said shrugging his shoulders. "You gon' be all right?"

Gus looked into the eyes that sometimes seemed to see right through people. He nodded his head toward Will.

Pursing his lips while scratching the back of his head Will nodded back in response. The unspoken responses between the two boys was seemingly enough.

"Night then Gus," Will said quietly. "Look out fo' yo-self now, Okay," his last words trailed off before disappearing into the next room.

Gus said goodnight to his brother. His eyes following him at a glance as he left. He pondered Wills words before getting up and returning to finish up his final tasks. *Will knew,* he thought. *He had a sense of such things and always seemed to see further down the road than most folks.*

Looking around, taking one last picture in his mind, Gus slowly breathed in all the scents and aromas of home. A memory to keep and take with him before quietly leaving, early the next morning.

* * *

While it was still dark and long before the old red rooster crowed Gus was up and off. At the foot of the dirt and gravel driveway, the rustic metal mailbox, stood alone at the roadside. A gateway to and from home. The last passage to cross, before his journey began. He was twelve years old. Walking down the rural two-lane road, leaving everything he knew, where would he go at his age? He understood. The journey ahead wasn't going to be easy. Looking back, he took a last look, biting his lower lip to beat back the last bit of fear and separation anxiety running through him. Then turning away, he picked up his pace and continued walking, down the road and away.

AWAY

The road from home snaked its way for a few miles through and beyond the farms of people who knew him. Of those, who might wonder and question where he was headed, some were family. Once past these farms, the Mississippi landscape was fairly flat and could be seen far into the distance. He had traveled this road many times before in his comings and goings. It was nearing mid-morning. Soon Gus would be out of view of those that might recognize him, making inquiries he didn't have time for nor felt like answering.

The next few days he kept on the move, sleeping out in the open air. He and his brothers often did this at home on the farm, so it was not a difficult adjustment. Luckily for him, while the Mississippi days were pretty hot and humid, the nights where he grew up were not that harsh. He had to be careful of snakes that crawled out at night looking for something warm to slither up next to. More than once he saw one of them winding across the road in the early morning or those that lay dead having been run over trying to make the crossing.

Not knowing where his next meal would come from and finding fresh water was a challenge all its own. Gus had only packed enough to last for a few days and soon realized he needed to ration what he had to make it last. Wild game was difficult to snag without a rifle. Once he caught a wild rabbit along the way, but that was rare. Outsmarting rabbits was no easy chore. His aim was good that day and the rabbit was…unlucky. He skinned it, cooked it and ate the whole thing that night. The rabbit was small and he was very hungry.

After a week or more of travel, his feet ached increasingly from all the constant walking in shoes not made for long journeys. Several times, he had to stop to pull them off to tend to his sore feet and give them a rest. Soaking them whenever he could find a cool stream.

As Gus journeyed on the days and nights passed before him. He worked the occasional odd jobs he could find along the way. "Need some help suh?" Was his calling card. It made him enough, to buy food and an occasional cold Coca-Cola or his other favorite orange soda pop along the way. Back then twenty-five cents went a long way.

Tending the farm from early morning to late nights had taught Gus to be industrious. Now, it was paying off as it helped him to find odd jobs along the way. His anger and hurt upon his departure had stayed with him and had yet to subside. He was resolved to make it on his own. Whether such stubbornness was his way of proving his independence to himself or to his mother it kept him going and determined. It had served him well and helped him survive. Once he completed and was paid for his work he left soon afterwards. Never did he stay long enough to get close to anyone. So far, he had no reason to regret that. His mistrust of other people, especially white folks, kept him at a safe distance.

The farther he traveled from home, the landscape began to change. It was dryer, becoming less green. Stopping roadside, he noticed a white farmer and several others hurrying to finish their crop picking. A family sized farm, it was small in comparison to some he had seen. The farmhouse was set back from the road about a quarter mile. Most of the farming land to be seen lay in front of the house between the road and the farmhouse. There were rows and rows of peas to be picked stretching out before him.

"You need help suh?" Gus asked.

After sizing Gus, up. The man replied. "Gotta get these picked today." If you can keep up, I'll pay you come sundown," the farmer replied.

Picking peas, he was no stranger to. He rolled back his sleeves and joined in. "yes suh."

There was a boy a few years older than Gus, the owner's son he later found out, who picked peas near him. A young girl bearing water, closer to Gus's age, brought a bucket and ladle to and fro for those who thirsted. Seeing the family resemblance, he thought she might be the boy's sister.

Everyone was rushing to finish so he bore down to match their pace. It was hot and he could feel the sweat bead up on his head.

He glanced to see the water bearer providing a ladle full to her brother and turned back to grab a handful of pea pods.

"Watter?" He heard and turned around to see her close, placing the ladle right under his mouth.

Did they know he was black, he wondered, *was it a test?*

She motioned for him to drink.

He finally accepted and drank, not wanting to make a scene. He drank a little and gave it back to her.

Placing her hand on his shoulder "You can have mo'," she said. Her Mississippi accent sang out to him.

His gut reaction to her touch was to take a step backward but he planted his feet and fought his urge to take flight. "Thank you, miss." He said politely, careful not to maintain prolonged eye contact. Back home, he only ran into the local white town folk while in town and then only in passing. Never was he alone...like now. Black and white did not socialize, existing in two separate worlds. In the south, black males knew, *keep your distance from white females, and keep your eyes to yourself.* It was knowledge learned through years of scattered history. A history littered with the terrible consequences of failing to recognize that unwritten tenet.

His body tingled uncomfortably and he felt odd. Rubbing his hands up and down his pants leg he tried to rid himself of his discomfort. She had made him nervous and ill at ease. He still couldn't tell what was going on here. Drinking from the same water container as white folks was not something you did and lived. He didn't want any misunderstandings. But if he turned her down or ignored her he might have to explain himself and attract unwanted attention.

Gus felt eyes watching him and didn't know what to say. He did know having her so close was not a good thing. *First the watter, now this girl* he thought. *Trouble waiting ta' happen. The white folks lynching kinda trouble.* "Ah betta gets back ta picking," he said with a polite smile, not wanting to be rude. Lowering his gaze, he picked up his pace. "Thank you fo' the watter." He said as he pushed to finish his task, and hoped he hadn't offended her. He knew one word from her, whether true or not, could quickly put an end to his journey. Once she'd riled the menfolk it'd be too late. They'd want blood. The risk to life and limb was too much to chance.

Gus worked his way up and down the row of Peas. The newly prickling sensation in his fingers gave him a bad feeling about this place. He rubbed his hands up and down his pants leg to rid himself of the feeling, but it persisted. *If he quit he wouldn't get paid,* he contemplated. *If he was to run, for sure they'd be after him just because he ran.* In the end, Gus pushed aside his feelings but kept a watchful eye about as he continued filling his basket with peas. But he knew he had to be ready for anything.

As the workday ended Gus saw two black field hands arrive from the far field. They served themselves drinking water... and from a different bucket. He knew then they must've thought he was white. For Gus, no matter what he looked like, he was Negro. To white folks and by law, one drop of black blood[1] was enough to make him guilty on all counts.

Once he was paid he thanked them and hurried away from there quickly, hoping to never see them again. If those white folks knew they had drank water from the same ladle as someone black they would turn on him. And who knew what the girl might do or say. The sweat flowed freely from his brow. He wiped it away with the sleeve of his shirt. But he knew as he left there it was not the heat nor the work that was making him sweat. There was trouble here, and the words rang out in his mind, *son, go the other way*.

---

[1] Wikipedia - Applied to no other group other than American blacks.

The **one-drop rule** is a social and legal principle of racial classification that was historically prominent in the United States in the 20th century: first in Tennessee in 1910 and in Virginia under the Racial Integrity Act of 1924. It asserted that any person with even one ancestor of sub-Saharan African ancestry ("one drop" of black blood) is considered black (*Negro* in historical terms).

People and places were few and far in-between after that. On the road for several days, he had counted the sun rise and set six days since. With no work, his supplies were starting to dry up. What's more, he had run dry of drinking water the day before. The very rural areas he had chosen to travel offered little certainty in the way of finding work. The dry, dusty landscape meant water was also scarce. Reluctantly, he approached a white farmer who had a well, which meant water and asked him for some work.

It was hot and humid that day but he was busy and the time went by quickly. Nearly finished with the chores the farmer assigned him, Gus stopped to get some water at the well. The old farmer had worked him hard but he needed money. The additional possibility of getting a meal made it worth-while. He filled his two water Jars and packed one into his knapsack for the journey ahead. Gulping down the water from the second jar, he wiped the sweat from his face onto his sleeve. Tired he closed his eyes taking in a long deep breath and set the jar of water down nearby. Before he recognized the danger he was in, the old farmer crept up behind him and held him firmly in his grasp. He struggled hard, but could not free himself.

"Be still now, boy," came the harsh voice behind him. The old farmer managed to tie him up and strap him to a post in little or no time, with his back exposed. Being so close, the stale rotting smell of liquor was all over the old man. His eyes had lost any trace of the warmth he saw initially. He was different now, the expression on his face seemed colder, meaner. The next thing he knew he was being whipped across his back with an old leather strap. The old man whipped him until his back was raw. In between his yelps, the belt hissed through the air slicing his back. Gus couldn't see it but felt his back swell up where the strap hit him.

Crack! Crack! Crack!

As the belt hit him, again and again, he managed a silent plea, *God Please!* At that moment Gus feared the worst and missed home, as never before. He was afraid. Afraid he might never see it again.

In the end, whether the old farmer tired of beating him or was too drunk to continue is unknown. On that night, he turned out to be no more than a sadist. Gus, at last, managed to get away with a few injuries as souvenirs.

While escaping in the dark Gus grabbed money from the shelf, that he thought was due him. As he ran away into the night he reached back to feel the sensitive spots he couldn't see. The welts in some places were too tender to touch causing him to wince. Other spots he felt were caked with dried blood and were starting to heal over. The pain would always be a reminder. Gus's distrust, however, had once again been given reason. "No. Ah won't trust em' no mo'," he said. Letting his guard down just that once had given him a back full of scars as reasons and a reminder why to never let it down again.

As Gus hastily made his way from his run-in with the old man he decided it might be best to stick to townships with more people. If he could find a safe one. Some towns had severe punishment for Negroes who got caught there after sundown. But he knew if something happened to him at one of these out of the way places, nobody would ever know. The dark and lonely Mississippi roads at night could be unforgiving. It was painful, the lessons being on your own taught, but he was learning. Nature can be cruel. Those that don't learn from their mistakes are weeded out by evolution, possibly never to live out their full lives. His survival depended on not making the same costly mistakes.

It wasn't until much later and after some distance that he realized the money, he grabbed as he ran away was over two-hundred dollars. He knew that he couldn't go back and there was no way to square it.

A few days later, Gus found a town that appeared somewhat hospitable to him. Upon his arrival, he took note of the posted, *whites only* and *colored area* signs, and avoided such places. Though he couldn't read, he recognized them by sight. Most towns had them, even his own. They caused him to question whether it might not be better to move on. Gus rarely saw another Black person there those first few days and quietly acknowledged the ones he did. Being Black in the White segregated world that was 1930's

Mississippi could feel like being the hunted. Being on your own made you easy prey. You had to be on constant watch for those who might decide you were just that, their prey, and he didn't feel like being prey. The laws favored white folks and rarely offered protection for those like him. He knew he could never let his guard down. Something about the place, however, overrode his uncertainties and Gus decided he might stay around. Just for a while.

Soon after, he landed a job at a local store where the owner paid him a fair wage and seemed not unsympathetic to his plight. Arriving early to work daily, he kept his head and eyes down, sweeping the floors, stocking the shelves and tried not to stand out. It seemed to work. But Gus knew that could easily change. The thought that the people in town might quickly turn on him once they realized he was black, remained and kept him cautious and ever alert. Over time his hard work and efforts gained him the respect and backing of the store's owner, Mr. Bill Pinckney. Everyone in town just called him Mr. Bill, and his support was good enough for Gus to get through most days.

It was said by those who knew them, that his mom's side of the family had the gift of sight. A sixth sense, that could pierce the world of the visible to things unseen. Such gifts were revealed in different ways and at different times for each family member. Traveling alone; especially at night, one has to be alert to changes and acutely aware of one's surroundings. To be able to sense invisible dangers that lurk and may pose a threat. It's a matter of survival. Normal senses are heightened when in survival mode. He began to recognize the warning, that sometimes flushed over his body, heightening his senses, alerting him. Gus's survival instincts started to work in his favor as he began to take heed. Abnormal sounds, movements, and even silences put him on instant alert.

It had been some time, several months since he had begun his journey. While taking stock of his earnings one night he counted and discovered that he'd accumulated almost four hundred dollars from his work and travails. This was a near fortune in 1930's Mississippi. Mr. Bill helped, offering him extra work for extra money when he needed things done. Word of his industriousness spread. Gus soon acquired jobs away from the store, helping out the locals and adding to his work efforts. He worked long hours, some nights getting to his campsite very late with few hours left to sleep. Often awaking those mornings disoriented not knowing when or where he was. It could take several moments to clear the fog and regain his sense of time and place. The money he made from the extra jobs he hid and stored away in a secret place.

* * *

As his anger subsided, he found himself remembering. His mind would visit home, vividly seeing the smiles and laughs on the faces of his brothers, sisters, and mama, sitting around the dinner table. The smile the memories brought soon disappeared at the sound of the brass bell above the store door, ringing as someone entered. Ding-a ling-ling. The breeze, that fanned through, blew away any memories that lingered in Gus's mind and served to remind him of just how far-off home really was. Pangs of home occurred more frequent as of late, especially when life was quiet. As tired as his various jobs caused him to feel, the separation pains he felt when he was alone made for some restless nights. Several months had passed since his arrival in town, and Gus had to admit to himself how much he missed them all.

* * *

Back home his family was going through hard times of their own. Many mouths to feed and a bad farming year had taken its toll. It was only being together as a family that got them through most hungry nights. But it was not without tribulations. Survival did not come without a cost. School was put on hold for a time for all who attended in favor of helping out on the farm.

"They's growin' slo'," Will said as he rubbed the leaves of the drying corn stalks between his fingers. "Needs mo' water." He dug his fingers into the flaky ground. Wait a few mo' days." He said to his youngest brother Hank Lee, as the others gathered around. "Gotta make it last y'all." Shaking his head slowly and muttering under his breath. His eyes were as wide as quarters. "We gon' lose a lot." They all gathered together moving row by row to remove the dead plants so the rest could survive.

It had been a dry season, and of the crops they depended upon, nearly half had failed. It not only meant a loss of money needed to buy things they could not grow but less food to go around the table.

On the days she worked, cooking or helping to clean with Lily, Addie, rose early to make breakfast. Fixing grits, biscuits and what few eggs the hens laid, before she headed out, leaving Will in charge. She found it hard to concentrate as of late and felt the emotional loss of her eldest child. The realization that she had indeed pushed him away weighed on her. He had been gone a good while now. Not knowing his whereabouts, she was uncertain of his return or even if he was okay.

* * *

Gus, almost thirteen now, had learned much about himself. He could survive on very little, eating only when his hunger demanded it. Cornbread, a filling meal all its own was a staple in the South at most southern tables during mealtimes. He stocked up whenever it was offered to him on any one of his various jobs. Fresh fruit he found to and from work, though he was careful not to eat the green, unripe ones. They made his stomach hurt. Nuts, pecans mostly and sometimes black walnuts, he found growing in the wild. He took advantage of those as well when he could. Often, he worked throughout the day snacking on whatever he had brought to work. Sometimes Mr. Bill, the store owner, would bless him with a hot meal.

"Gus, come on over here. Sit down and eat now. Missus Pinckney made extra today," he would say.

At first hesitant, he refused but eventually accepted. He ate sparingly, never eating more than Mr. Bill did. With time, trust and a little cajoling from Mr. Bill, that changed.

"You can eat more than that now, Gus. Go on now… eat up," he said

So, he ate until his belly was filled.

He also learned something that would become a trademark of his as he grew into adulthood. He was a saver, putting any extra money he made aside. It was a character quality he developed, one he would hold onto throughout his life. As the oldest of his siblings, Gus was often the one assigned to take the lead on tasks and chores. It made him unfaltering and certain in his decisions-a rare thing for someone his age.

He was happy, mostly, with his work. It kept him busy, filling his time from sunup to sundown.

Thoughts of home again began to hound him, telling him something was missing.

Biting into a piece of fried chicken Mr. Bill's wife had prepared took him instantly home. He momentarily froze, a faraway look in his eye. *Taste like Mama's*, he thought.

He was at a crossroads now. He could continue to work and save for his future, cutting himself off from his past. But if he stayed the course he could lose all that he was–his family, his history, everything that tied him to this world. Tossing and turning at the end of a long day, he chased after thoughts and memories of home.

Visiting him, one night a dream came to him he could not seem to make sense of. Heading up the road back toward home, he could almost see, smell and taste it in front of him. An eerie feeling coursed through his body, stopping him from going forward. As he approached, the grass, plants and everything green on the land seem to shrivel up, turning to a dried-up faded brown. The land was dying before his eyes. The dream startled him awake, making him sit straight up. Twice the same dream came to him. Sleep evaded him on both nights. The feelings invoked would not go away. Was it a dream, he wondered, or something else? *Will would know* he thought *but Will's not here.*

Over time, the sleepless nights, caused by the good memories and the dreams both good and bad, began taking their toll. Gus's eyes had begun to look red and tired lately.

Mr. Bill noticed the dreariness and dark circles growing under his eyes and questioned him. "Not much sleep huh Gus?" he asked, catching him off guard.

"Naw suh." he straightened up. "Got something in my eye, ah think," Gus replied rubbing his eye with his free hand.

Mr. Bill just nodded, dragging the words out, "Uh huh" at his questionable answer.

Stretching and reaching his arms skyward, he yawned hard. He knew he could only use the *got something in my eye excuse* with Mr. Bill for so long. Looking around, he yawned again and quickly straightened up thinking *especially if he was ta' catch me doing this.* Seemed like with his schedule lately, he couldn't help it though. In the end, Gus could be alone here, working toward some futures end or eat his pride and go home. After another long, sleepless night, he determined home it would be. *A little more savings and his journey home could begin* he thought. He had left them all without a word. Hopefully, he was missed as much as he missed them. But it didn't matter at this point; he missed and needed his family.

The job at the local store was a good fit, but there was one particular source of concern and irritation that visited the store from time to time. A young white boy, a year or two older than him, would come into the store on occasion and ruffle his feathers to no end. Jeb! Jeb never called Gus by his given name, referring to him insultingly as *Sunshine*. It was always, "Whatcha got there, Sunshine?" or "Whatcha doin' today Sunshine?"

Gus gritted his teeth when he first heard the word. It made him wince, his body tightening. He hesitated, then corrected him. "Gus. My name is Gus," he told Jeb pointedly, but to no avail.

"Ok... Sunshine." Jeb replied, exaggerating his comment, smirking and brushing off his words as if they meant nothing.

"You watch yourself now Jeb," Mr. Pinckney cast a watchful glare at Jeb after noticing his ongoing interest in Gus, cautioning him as he exited.

Observing Jeb, Gus wondered what he wanted but doubted it was anything good for him. His heart beat faster, feeling it thump, thump, thump, under his shirt. Was Jeb making fun of him at his expense or did he actually know what he was saying? He for sure recognized the meaning and off-color slur the word carried. Shine! Sunshine! If you were black and from the south, you knew them. Not wanting any trouble after finally finding a place to settle, he calmed down and thought it better to pay him no mind. Soon he would be heading home.

Jeb on the other hand, continued his bothersome ways whenever he came to the store. He made a point to greet him on the sly with "Hey *Sunshine*." Like a stalker, he kept a keen eye on Gus for his reaction.

Gus went about his daily duties as if it didn't matter. *If he could deal with that stubborn ol' mule of theirs he could handle Jeb,* he thought.

Though he would never show his discomfort openly, whenever Jeb was around, the taunting felt like an extra weight he had to carry. His body stiffened, reflexively on its own, and his fingers would tingle at Jeb's nearing presence, putting him on alert and on his toes. He found his attention drawn toward the door, often looking to it just before Jeb entered the store. It was unsettling, but he was able to keep his eye on him that way.

Bearing the insults, he figured learning to deal with Jeb was one of his life lessons, *some people ya just can't be nice too,* he thought. He tried with Jeb, he really did. But Jeb was a bully, and he took pleasure in taunting Gus... just because, as much as he could reckon. Lately, Jeb seemed to visit the store more often, either having nothing better to do, or for some purpose all his own.

The store owner, Mr. Bill initially instructed Gus, "Pay Jeb no mind Gus. Go bout' your business" Over time, however, that sentiment changed. He felt a growing need to keep Jeb an arm's length distance from Gus whenever he entered the store. He ran Jeb out if he hovered around too long without buying anything. "You ain't buying? Ya gotta go, Jeb. You got a home! Go on now, go on!" Mr. Bill even threatened to ban Jeb, several times, from the store if he didn't learn to control himself.

One day, at his limit Mr. Bill pulled Gus aside. Jeb was getting more out of control lately, and he was growing wary of him. "Man-to-man, Gus ... I can only look out for you while you're here at the store," he said earnestly. "I can't guarantee your safety elsewhere. I've noticed Jeb's been skulking about, watchin' as you leave work and it's bothersome. I just can't protect ya away from here."

"Yessuh, I know," Gus said. "Ah've seen him too a few times, following and sneaking aroun' behind me. But so far ah've been able to shuck him off."

"You are a pretty hard-working young fella Gus," he said placing a hand on Gus's shoulder. Though you never much say, I have to wonder, where yo' family is. Something's missing from your life. It ain't too hard to figure. Not sleeping much lately, bags under yo' eyes, yo' mind elsewhere. Definite giveaways for someone who notices," he said.

The right corner of Gus's mouth twisted upward into a sheepish, *I'm busted*, half smile, "Yessuh." he replied.

"I'd suggest if you have a place to go to, this might be a good time to make your way there before something bad happens." Mr. Bill put his hand to his chin. He was quiet as if he had to ponder his next words. "I hate to lose ya, Gus. Gotten used to having you aroun' here. But can't say I really trust that Jeb. He might try and do something. No tellin' with him."

"Thank You, Mr. Bill," Gus said. I will think about it, Suh, and decide tonight. If I don't make it back here in da morning, well... you'll know I'm gone then." A wave of emotion welled up in him unexpectedly and he wiped away the sudden moisture from his eyes with his shirt sleeve. Choking up, the lump in his throat made it hard to swallow. He turned quietly toward the door, having found it hard to get the words out. He had become close to this man who had shown him more kindness than his real father ever had. That night, as he left the store, saying goodnight, he decided it was indeed time to go home.

LOOSE ENDS

Gus began to make his way back to where he set up camp during his stay in town.

He walked in a daydream of sorts, each step giving way to anxious and eager feelings, bringing him closer to the family homecoming that was on his mind.

The space he had chosen to camp was a small open setting surrounded by trees and bushes. Not far away, a small creek streamed that carried fresh water. Surprisingly, he never ran into anyone at the creek during his time there. There was a minor rock crest that housed a small cave, and in the cave, was a large rock, resting atop his savings. The rock required leverage to move, which he did with a fulcrum created by a smaller rock and a hefty branch. His savings were wrapped in a sturdy old rawhide material to keep the moist ground from damaging it. He would need to pack and head out while he still had some light.

As he continued his way to his campsite, instinctively he glanced about more than usual, casting a cautious eye every few feet or so. He had heard nothing, but he had that creepy tingly feeling that he had come to know as a warning. Yet, after taking another wide slow scan of the area, he saw nothing that might be cause for alarm. The feeling, however, persisted, like a small flickering flame, fighting to come to life. It would not go away. He sensed something was out of place. It put him on edge, and he moved ahead, perched on the balls of his feet and on-guard.

It was nearing dusk now, and he was losing light. Arriving, he began gathering and packing his belongings. Lastly, he grabbed the sturdy branch used to move the huge rock to unearth and grab his savings. He gave a hard push downward nearly lifting him off his feet. The large boulder moved but was being difficult today. One last push. He jumped up throwing his full weight down on the branch. It snapped propelling him backwards, but it had lasted long enough to move the heavy rock one last time. He scrambled to where his stash lay and scooped it up. Once he had it in hand he sat and added in his most recent earnings to his knapsack. He quickly stitched it closed with the needle and thread he kept for repairing his clothing. Then he rubbed it with dirt to hide the new stitches. *It is too quiet,* he thought. *No birds, no crickets… no nothing. It's as if they took the night off.*

Finally, he was all packed and was ready to set off toward the road for home when he heard a noise.

Crack!

Swerving quickly, his back stiffened and his eyes raced toward the direction of the sound. The faint highlights of a lone dim figure slowly emerged from the bushes into view. Fingers tingling, his head ringing, he strained to see who it was.

The shadow loomed large momentarily and began to take shape. Jeb, stood there emerging into the light, boldly glaring at him, smirking a disdainfully superior grin. The look on his face gave away his bad intentions. He had been clever, waiting for Gus to put all his things together.

"I knew you was out here somewhere, hidin' something, Sunshine." Jeb stabbed that last word at him as if it was a knife he wanted to plunge into his body. "Hand it over, nigger." He spat out. "It's mine now."

With that last pronouncement, he now knew what Jeb's true intent had been from the beginning. Days spent suffering through Jeb's insults, had brought them both here. "You didn't earn this, Jeb," Gus spoke, "I worked awfully hard fo' this money." His shoulders drooped, giving the appearance of air escaping a deflating balloon. "But alright." Slowly, he reached out and handed the sack over towards Jeb.

"Ow! That hurt!" Jeb howled as Gus jabbed the sewing needle deep into his hand and he dropped the knapsack, shaking his hand rapidly as if that might ease the pain.

He glared at Gus. "I'm gonna hurt you, boy." Springing forward, he leapt at Gus and was on top of him in an instant. Being older and larger, he quickly overpowered Gus, pinning both his hands with his own. He took that moment to gloat. "You mine now, boy," he said as he grabbed Gus by the face twisting his hand back and forth over it squeezing torturously.

Turning his head quickly and just enough, Gus bit down hard on Jeb's hand.

"Eeeyow!" Jeb yelped shrieking loudly like a wounded animal, momentarily putting him off balance.

Reaching out Gus grabbed a loose rock and swung it hard at Jeb's head. The dull thud as the rock connected sent Jeb sprawling awkwardly, grabbing his head and landing on his back.

He looked up at Gus who was now standing, "I'm gonna get you boy, and that their money is mine..." His last word faded as he passed out and keeled over, blood dripped down the side of his head. He lay there quiet, motionless.

Gus looked bewildered, "Oh, God! Did Ah kill 'im?" He put his hands to his face. A sick woozy feeling overcame him, and he had to fight the dizzying urge to throw up.

Jeb was not moving. Gus sat there momentarily stunned. The world around him seemed to go still and silent. A black man who killed a white man would have no place to hide in this world. He couldn't go home now, maybe never! What should he do? As he sat there frozen, contemplating his fate, he heard a noise, a cough. He looked hopefully and then was frightened as Jeb's body jerked, then flopped briefly like fish out of water. Then his thrashing halted and Jeb took in a deep wheezing lungful of air and began to breathe. He lay there, still unmoving but apparently, alive.

Tearing off a piece of Jeb's shirt, he wrapped it around his head to control the bleeding. Taking a moment, he slowly poured water into Jeb's mouth to make sure he was all right. Jeb's unfocused eyes moved slowly.

Jeb reached up, grabbing Gus firmly by the wrist and with a wry smile, said, "Boy!" Finally relaxing and releasing his grip, he lay there, eyes open.

Gus quickly grabbed everything that had scattered during his tussle with Jeb. Still wary, he glanced over his shoulder from time to time, to keep an eye on Jeb. Wanting to leave no trace of himself, he scanned the campsite area. He wasn't much worried that Jeb would tell. He figured Jeb was not the type to admit getting whooped, especially by him. But he did want to make sure he was okay. He was moving about, slowly, but on his own. The wind picked up suddenly, blowing the leaves around him. The surrounding trees, plants, bushes, and brush swayed, pointing him in the direction he needed to follow.

Run, the usually small voice in his mind now shouted.

He took one last look and then turned, and ran as fast as he could. His heart pumping fast he stumbled over the uneven terrain, rambling through bush and brush that nicked, scratched and poked him as he made his way toward the highway–the two-lane road that ran to the next town.

It was time to go home!

PERILOUS

The signposts are all around.
Woe to the person who does not take
heed their call!

Gus had stopped running for some time now but still walked at a brisk pace. His legs had grown heavy and his runny nose and constant sniffling was yet another sign of just how exhausted he was. His breath steady, he felt for the monies he kept hidden in the fold of the knapsack. He could barely feel where it was and hoped it was safe there. Thanks to his mom, he had learned to sew, mending clothes for himself and those of his younger brothers and sisters. It was a skill that had served him well on this journey. Tonight, that small needle may have saved his life.

He was tiring, drained from everything that had happened. Eyeballing a-ways down the road he could not see the end of it. "Can't stop now," he said. Knowing he had a-ways to go pressed him onward. He'd hitchhiked in the early part of his return journey but did so only during the day.

Initially, he had some luck and caught rides from some black travelers. They were short distance trips, but each one took him a bit closer to home. He was doing okay and making good time, but not enough to suit him. He wanted to put as much distance between himself and Jeb as he could.

* * *

He felt it before he saw or heard anything. The ringing sound inside his head began to chime.

It wasn't loud, but the volume was constant... and growing.

His hands and feet tingled lightly. The sound of an approaching vehicle caused him to glance back over his shoulder. He could hear the engine roaring, down to the putty, putty, idling sound the car made as it slowed.

A local sheriff's car drove up and inched past him then slowed, to mirror Gus's pace. The sheriff, his vehicle tires slowly crunching the roadside brush and stones, eyeballed him as he walked down the otherwise deserted road.

The baby hairs on his arm and back of his neck stood up as if statically charged. *Was it because a Jeb?* He wondered. *No, Ah think ah have come far enough.* Trying to hide any nervousness, he looked over, his hand shading his eyes and acknowledged the sheriff, nodding his head.

Hoping his wide-eyed expression was hidden enough to not cause him problems.

Returning the nod, the sheriff's watchful eye tracked him. Unsure of what else to say, he continued forward keeping his pace, wiping the sweat from his brow as needed. The sheriff had shadowed his movements, giving him a scrutinizing stare, before reaching up and touching the brim of his hat. Then, just as quickly he turned away, revved up his engine and sped off down the road.

When he could see the Sheriff's car was no longer in view, Gus breathed a sigh of relief. In his mind, that Sheriff had looked an awfully lot like an older Jeb. Coincidence or his imagination he didn't know which. He did know that these sheriffs asked too many questions. Though he had done nothing wrong they were not known for helping people like him.

He could hear Grandpa's voice in his head, clear as day. He was very young and Grandpa was still alive then. In town to visit a friend of grandpa's they watched local sheriffs in a nearby black part of town, stopping several black men.

Shaking his head, Grandpa commented. "These heah' Law folks, Sheriffs, Klan, all come from the same place." Holding Gus's hand, he squeezed, adding, "The slave patrols. In the ol' days they captured slaves and freed black folks alike for money. Doing whatever they felt like to the folks they caught. Not everyone lived," he said sighing. Same folks are the sheriff and police around here now." Don't much care bout' us." His steely eyes looked on intently at the scene unfolding before them. "Not much changed since then," Grandpa said. "No one stopped em' then... and no one stops em' now." Averting their eyes, they were careful not to make any lingering eye contact. Grandpa's voice was frustrated and angry as they stepped quickly on their way lest they got stopped and became the next targets. "Any ol' Negro would do." He said cynically to Gus. Grandpa's last warning as they walked away brought him back to the present. "You never know which one is which, klan, sheriff's, the law or if they be one and the same. Be careful when they're around. They's trouble and If you see trouble coming... head the other way, Gus."

Gus understood. *If they really were bad ones, you might not know until it was too late. They might try to take away my money or worse.*

Now he knew. There was no more time to waste, he had to get as far away from here as he could. That fear pressing in on him made him less cautious.

* * *

It was high noon and hot. The thick and humid midday heat beat heavily upon him. His shirt was soaked and he had walked for hours when he accepted a ride from two white males, in their thirties.

"Where ya heading boy?" they asked him.

"Home suh'. A little farther down the road," he told them.

"We going down the road. Get in." The man on the passenger side replied, emotionless.

Jumping into the back-seat, glad not to suffer the heat, the breeze from the partially rolled down window was pleasant. The breeze, however, seemed to be playing tricks with him, whispering, a sound, a word. He couldn't quite make it out. Again, *something... full.* He ignored the high piercing sound that began whistling like a teapot in his head, warning him away–a warning this time that was more than a flicker it was a flame ignited, surging to life. He chose to pay them no mind.

At first, he was fine, and the two men seemed amiable enough. After a while, though he could tell something about them was off. Their words and actions seemed a little rehearsed.

"How far is you really goin' boy?" The passenger side male asked. His, sleepy looking eyes hiding his increasingly dark demeanor.

Their talk and their questions soon grew more antagonistic. The frequent silent looks between them made him increasingly uncomfortable. He knew he had made a mistake. The once tingling feeling had turned prickly, coursing through him like a thousand small needles jabbing into his body all at once.

Again, the wind whispered to him. This time he understood it. *Careful!*

Then, with a quick, sharp turn, the driver turned and barreled off the main road onto a bumpy dirt pathway, that jostled him around. It took him further from his path home.

He feared the worst and tried to push the door open, but could not. The window opening was too narrow to offer him any chance of escape. *Only to come this far,* he thought.

The two men hurled all types of verbal abuses at him but he kept his temper in check and pressed himself tightly in the corner against the right-side door. They toyed with him at their leisure for the next few miles as they headed down the old road into darkness.

The driver with his strange half-closed eyelids gave him a sleepy but calculating appearance. He hadn't caught it before. He looked as if he might be the one calling the shots. He nodded or grunted and the other man would react as if his leash had been loosened.

"You lied to us, boy!" The passenger side male cackled looking back at him. His eyes danced wildly with excitement, something not there before.

He appeared to take enjoyment in taunting Gus. Something about the man was off. He had an air of danger and unpredictability. It made Gus uncertain of how much trouble he might be in. But he understood enough to know that this guy might turn on him like a wild animal at any moment. It kept him on edge and anxious as he tried to figure out the next moves in their game. He had seen similar behavior in cats that played with their prey before deciding its final fate.

Gus's head throbbed as the warning in his head grew intensely, shrieking loudly. If Jeb's warning was like a flicker, this one was a full-on surge of burning fire that beat at the walls of his mind, numbing his limbs and paralyzing his body. Cupping his hands, he put the fingers of both hands to his forehead to try and relieve the pressure. Faintly he could hear a distant voice.

"Hear me." Then the words, "Can you hear me boy!" screamed out at him.

Shocked out of his daze, he saw a hand reaching towards him. He reacted, but not quickly enough as the man in front of him reached back quickly and snatched his knapsack from his hand. *My money!* He thought to himself, as he flinched away. The fear in his eyes appeared to motivate and give them a twisted satisfaction. The men wore self-satisfied, crooked sneers, visible on both their conniving faces. The one with his knapsack rummaged through it, obviously looking for something.

Wide-eyed and frozen in place, Gus's twitching eyes watched him, desperately hoping they wouldn't look too deep.

The man rifled hurriedly through Gus's belongings, taking his small food stash and a couple of loose coins he was able to dig out. He shook them inside his closed fist, clinking and rattling next to his ear, before pocketing the coins, smiling. At long last, seemingly satisfied with their newly acquired booty, the outwardly unstable man threw his knapsack back toward him, just missing his face.

They had driven this small dark road for a while now. Miles out of his way, they had taken him and he still did not know what they had in mind for him. The brakes squealed, and the car slowed down. Gus tensed, scrunching and pressing himself tightly against the rear door, not sure what might be next.

Finally, the car stopped, and the man in front of him got out and opened the rear door next to where Gus sat. Grabbing him forcibly, he threw Gus to the ground. Gus held onto his knapsack. He hit the ground rolling and came to a stop against a wall of bushes. Righting himself, he waited for their next move as he contemplated fight or flight. But he knew he couldn't win a fight.

The volatile lone male, stood staring at him unmoving as if waiting for Gus to make the first move. Motionless, Gus crouched low, staring back, shaking hands pressed against the ground– at the ready to spring to flight if he had to. Long tense moments passed as the two of them sized each other up. In the end, unexpectedly, the man turned around without so much as a word, got into the front seat, and the car drove off.

They could have taken his life, he would later recount to his future wife. *Others,* he thought, *maybe had not been so lucky.* In particular, it was difficult for a black child traveling alone and on the road during those tumultuous times. Especially in the world that was then Mississippi and America in the South. The tormenting incident was maybe the one time he could remember appreciating having a white father and looking as he did.

He was at once thankful, but fear soon followed and surged over him in waves. Taking in a series of short breaths before exhaling one long breath, he wept, not out loud but silently, falling to his knees. After a while, he gathered himself. Wiping the tears from his eyes, his nerves calmed, his breathing returned to normal. He was grateful. He knew how fortunate he was that he still had his savings and his life.

Emotionally spent, and physically exhausted he determined he would walk the rest of the way. It was dark though, and seeing where to go was going to be difficult.

He learned something, that day. Another life-lesson. Never make a critical decision under stress and in a hurry. And always, always take heed of that piercing shrill cautioning sound that went off in his head, serving to warn him of danger. He was still miles away from home, but he was not going to take any more unnecessary chances with people he didn't know.

For now, he had to get a move on, in case his abductors changed their mind and came back to continue their game.

Walking all night, feeling and sensing his way through the darkness, his eyes gradually became accustomed to the shade of night. His ears were perked for any sound hinting of would be dangers. There was no clear-cut path. Several times he was put on guard as moving creatures slid or ran across his feet. Once he stepped on something that squealed and ran off into the night. He felt it nip at his pant leg as it passed, but luckily, he was not bitten.

In the end, it was one of nature's tiniest creatures, a tiny lightning bug, that came to his rescue and helped him through his dilemma. Lighting his way like a journeying beacon he trailed it through the darkness that night.

* * *

Back home on the farm, his brothers and sisters were worried for him. He had been gone a long time, and his whereabouts were unknown. All missed him, but Addie and Will visibly seemed to worry for him most. Will had carried a gaunt expression on his face the past several days. It had not gone unnoticed.

They had heard word of sightings of Gus in faraway small towns but never knew for sure if the rumors were true. They had no proof.

Will by all accounts, had been born with a strong sense, a sixth sense of things unseen. A family gift that seemed to have concentrated more intensely in young Will than any of his other siblings. His foresight had prevented harmful things from happening to those he cared for on more than one occasion. But his visions came at a cost. It was a terribly heavy burden to see and carry around things that no one else could see. It weighed on him, especially now. Such incidents, when they did happen, however, were kept tightly wrapped within the family circle.

Will was plagued repeatedly of late by a host of waking visions and night dreams about his older brother. Those visions of Gus's woes haunted him, and he was doubly troubled.

Suffering through the sleepless nights, he kept his fears to himself. His feelings however traveled through his family members like the flow of an electric current that was felt by all. All any of them could do was wait and hope.

HELP

Fate again stepped in after he reached the main road back toward home. A few miles into his journey as he walked down the road, his pace began to slow under the hot and humid Mississippi heat. Unexpectedly, he ran into a black farmer from a small town near his hometown area.

The farmer at first drove past him, but his old beat up dingy black pickup truck slowed down, pulling over to the roadside. "Ya'll need a ride?" he asked lightheartedly, looking back from his driver's side window.

It was good to see another Black face but Gus's mistrust was on high alert. His last experience had taught him to take caution with anyone he didn't know. He could hear two battling voices at odds in his mind. *Be careful! Don't trust him!* The voice proclaimed loudly. Then another voice shouted. *We need help, take the ride!* He didn't know which voice to trust. His senses once muted, when he began his journey were now heightened. Like a volume knob, they had been gradually dialed up, by each encounter along his journey. Closing his eyes, taking several quiet breaths to calm himself, he was soon at ease. There were no alarms. No warning shrill or tingling–only quiet.

Fighting his reflex urge to refuse the offer because of the fear and mistrust built up over the last few days, he accepted the traveler's offer for a ride. "Yes suh. Thank you," he answered, getting into the old pickup truck.

The road taken from there was not the most direct route because the farmer made several stops in small towns along the way at small stores and locales. Gus napped whenever the farmer made one of his stops and was away from the truck. He was not yet secure enough to fall asleep in the driver's presence. Somehow, sensing the farmer's return, he would awake on cue. Even with all the stopping and starting, Gus's long trek home was thankfully shortened by a few days—days that he would have otherwise had to journey on foot. He hadn't realized he had traveled so far.

Three days later, he arrived at the home of his birth.

* * *

It was nearing dusk as Will sat on the side porch his legs dangling over the side. Free from the haunting dreams that had tortured him on previous nights, he had at long last gotten a full night's sleep.

Turning sharply to his right he felt something touch his right shoulder. He saw nothing but sensed something. An abrupt chill in the air cut through the heat and ran past his body. It made him uneasy because he knew what followed. He felt a nudge in the middle of his back and leapt off the porch onto the ground. Visits from spirits were not new to Will. They had appeared to him for as long as he could remember. But they were not always familiar to him and not of his choosing. Looking straight out he got a whiff of his granddad's pipe as it drifted away from him. The familiar sweet aroma put him at ease and gave him comfort. Growing up, he and Gus, the two eldest had spent the most time with granddad before he passed. They both had distinct memories of him and his pipe. Following the familiar scent, he spotted a fleeting wisp of vapor. It hoovered before him, then grew fainter and melted into the rippling heat waves that shimmered just above the ground. He knew what he had to do, and continued following the smell of grandpa's pipe.

Stepping out from the side of the house, Will, looked to the front toward the direction he had been beckoned. He heard a faint noise. A truck. *It was close* he thought, but was growing distant and appeared to be moving away. He made his way to the front of the house. He was not alone.

* * *

Standing at the roadside the old mailbox, Rural Route 2 Box 2B, had maintained its post. A place it had held long since before his birth. A familiar piece of home, it seemed to greet Gus. He was never happier to see it. One deep breath and straightaway he began treading straight up the lightly graveled, dirt driveway. Gus soon emerged rising into view of his brothers and sisters. He strode straight upward until alas he stood in full view of those standing there to see who had arrived. Once they recognized him they rushed excitedly from the house, running and jumping from the porch to embrace him. Hank Lee, stumbled once but bounced right up in stride and didn't miss a step.

Addie, sticking her head out from inside the house to find out what all the fuss was about, recognized him and rushed from the porch to welcome him.

Amid the squeals of "Gus! Brother!" from his siblings, Addie grabbed and held onto him, squeezing tightly.

Seeing the tears in her eyes, for the first time in as far back as he could remember, he knew, she truly loved him. His brothers and sisters who had been so worried warmly welcomed him one and all. His fears about whether they missed him or not had been laid to rest.

Times had grown worse during his absence. The family farm had not done so well. As he surveyed he took note, viewing with concern as everyone surrounded and escorted him to the house. The decline was caused in equal parts because of the unusually dry season he had witnessed, and because of his absence. He was the oldest, the one who mostly took care of things. He flashed back to his reoccurring dream. The plants, grass, and crops shriveling up, turning green to brown. *It was all real.*

The family fussed over him like an honored guest. His giggling sisters, Rosa Mae and Mary Lou, taking him by both hands, called out "Come on now," their beautiful southern accents practically sang the words, "Ovah Heah." They directed him to sit down, on the old pillow lined, quilt-covered wooden bench that served as a sofa. The two youngest girls rushed away, and then quickly returned and offered him a big jar of freshly made ice cold sweet tea.

Addie, right behind them, brought out fresh made hot biscuits that had been baking and handed them to him.

"Thank you, Mama." Gus, gladly accepted what was offered. He nearly drank the entire, preserve jar full of cold sweet tea, finally stopping to catch his breath and bite into the warm moist biscuit, spread with freshly churned butter. "Uhmmm!" he said closing his eyes, savoring the taste. Having his mama's hot biscuits and sweet tea let him know he was truly home.

"There's not much else to give right now, Gus. "Addie's tone was apologetic, her eyes tried to hide the pain of worry. But he could see it.

He knew he had lost weight on his journey. The fit of his clothes told him so. But he also noted the overall thinning of his family members. Their clothes hung almost as loosely as his own did. He was glad he'd come back when he did. Gathering information from what he could see from the state of things, he could only guess their plight. Glancing down he took a quick look at the bag in his hand as if drawn to it. *Now was a good time* he thought. He smiled, looking up at his mom. Though she appeared happy, the burden she carried, and the worry lines on her face were evident. Reassuringly he reached out and touched Addie's arm until he had her attention. Then grabbing for his knapsack, setting it on his lap Gus pulled and tore at the stitching inside.

His family watched, wide-eyed, as he tore at his knapsack to open it. It was surprisingly resistant. Their strange reactive looks to each other seemed to indicate they might be wondering what was wrong with him.

Once he got to the hidden sweet spot, he smiled and paused to get a good grip. He strained, ripping hard and began to pull out the first assortment of old papers and clothing used for stuffing. Then came the first handfuls of what seemed to be an endless supply of dollars. He placed the first handful in his mother's hands, beaming with pride as he closed his hand over hers. He followed up by passing out handfuls to his astonished brothers and sisters, who were jumping up and down. Their gleeful sounds made him a little giddy and filled him with pride. Grinning, his face soon turned into a full, and deep throated laugh. Gus couldn't remember the last time he had seen them all so happy. Looking at their faces, cherishing that moment, he knew at last that this was his home, his family. He would not be leaving them again.

The tears and embraces he received when he arrived indicated they were just as happy to have him back. It was not just the money. After a long trip and back to the local store that evening, there were treats and many full bellies. There was a long celebration that night. They slept soundly afterwards, all except for Gus. He was happy and too excited to sleep right away. Having had to sleep outdoors for so long on his journey, it took him a while to relax and get comfortable. He finally fell asleep late that night, close to early morning, just hours before the sun rose. He did not awaken when the old rooster crowed. The others let him sleep and quietly tiptoed around him as he rested.

When he finally did arise that next day, the sun was high in the sky. He and Will took a tour of the farm to take stock of what could be done to help out.

"Good to have ya back brother," Will said patting his shoulder.

Gus nodded his head. "Good to be back Will."

From that day forth, he became, the man of the house. Until her death many years later, Addie relied on and trusted him most of all. He cared for her even after he had begun the next generation with his own family.

EPILOGUE

When my mother told me this story, I better understood my dad and why family was so important to him. I called him as soon as I could, and I began with an apology for my words spoken to him in anger.

My dad accepted my apology, "It's okay, Son," he said and apologized to me for his part in our disagreement as well. There were not a lot of words between us. It was our way. Just quiet acknowledgment and an understanding. But I could feel his quiet smile through the phone. Maybe he could feel mine too.

As I sat alone in my dorm room, I pondered his life and mine. I felt that I finally understood him, the man - the human being, his humanity, and why he may have taken our dispute so hard. Why it was that he had always pushed me so, to look out for my younger brother; to keep the bond between the two of us strong. We were the last remaining siblings at home. The others, much older, had long left the nest.

I was the eldest child. He and my Mom, both older, would one day be gone. As it was when he grew up, the eldest child bore responsibility for the younger ones. Even though I was leaving, no matter where I went, this was my family. I would always be connected. He was correct, and I was. It took me leaving in anger to figure that out. We never had one of those types of arguments again.

* * *

One day, when I was nearing adulthood, fourteen, almost fifteen years old, my father came home early from work, agitated and worried. He and my mother walked into their bedroom closed the door to have a long private talk.

She later told my younger brother and me that he had punched a man on his job and now was afraid he would be fired for it.

I asked her, "Why did he hit the man, Mama?"

My question was followed by a repeat question from my younger brother. "Yeah Mama, … why?" Lonzo asked.

Both of us standing there our eyes wide and mouths agape like two baby birds yearning to be fed the true story. What happened to Dad?

"The man at work had kept calling him names, and your dad had asked him to stop for some time." She said calmly. "It was not his name, and finally your dad just lost his temper."

"What did the man call him?" I asked curiously. My younger brother looked at me and to Mom, nodding his head up and down, acknowledging yes in agreement.

Mom looked at us with a look of knowing, no surprise or indication otherwise of emotion on her face. Her answer which I did not understand at the time was simply, "*Sunshine.* He kept calling your dad *Sunshine.*"

Though I did not wholly understand the implication of the word at the time, as my life became seasoned with my own experiences, it became clear.

My mother used to tell me I was a lot like him, strong-willed and proud. I often thought though that it was my younger brother who was more like him, in many ways.

Throughout my life, I have had regrets for doing things and not doing things. But I never have, and I never will regret being my father's son.

ABOUT THE AUTHOR

G. S. Willis

Born in the sleepy rural farmlands near Wesson, Mississippi, G.S Willis's parents migrated to Michigan when he was eight. His eighth-grade English teacher predicted a career for him as a writer. It was flattering, but at thirteen years old, he didn't take it too seriously.

At Michigan State University, his teachers encouraged him to pursue a writing career. He chose a Business degree. After graduation from Michigan State, G.S. moved to Los Angeles, CA, and attended film school. Film school was a supportive, creative environment and a chance to meet many people from various countries and cultures.

It was all about the stories. The class projects pushed us all to come up with fresh ideas constantly. It was a story generating factory; a place that sparked and encouraged creativity. His first year there, he won an award in an independent screenplay competition.

After film school was over, he worked for years in corporate America. Following several successful real estate deals he decided to strike out on his own; eventually returning to his creative roots and the things he enjoyed as a child.

His first project was a family storybook that included the histories and stories of his parents, and immediate family members. The stories he hoped would be a legacy to leave for current family members and future generations. The initial story about his dad, Gus, seemed to gain traction right away and soon took on a life of its own. It was then that he decided to listen to those voices that had encouraged him to walk the writing path.

Gus is the genesis story he feels. His mom's story, however, is an equally interesting one. He plans to complete it after Gus's book release. She was a remarkable woman with a near photographic memory. Her southern roots shaped us all. She used to tell me when I was younger, and unappreciative of her, "You're gonna miss me when I'm gone." Every day, she was so right!

Contact G.S. Willis

Via email: gs@gswillis.com

On the web: gswillis.com